DOLLY PEG PIRATES
Craft Book

TOP THAT™

Licensed exclusively to Top That Publishing Ltd
Tide Mill Way, Woodbridge, Suffolk, IP12 1AP, UK
www.topthatpublishing.com
Copyright © 2015 Tide Mill Media

Pirates!

Get ready to transform ordinary wooden dolly pegs into a collection of swashbuckling pirates!

It's easy!

Just follow the simple step-by-step instructions in this book and use the pattern templates on page 32 to get started.

Items you'll need

Buy your number one pirate component – dolly pegs – from craft and hobby shops, or online. You'll also need a selection of coloured tissue paper, fuzzy sticks and felt-tip pens or crayons as part of your pirate-making kit, plus some other items. Make sure you have glue and scissors at hand for all your projects.

Check out the list at the beginning of each project and gather everything together before you start. That means you'll be ready to get making straight away!

Preparing tissue paper and templates

Every project uses a piece of tissue paper measuring 30 x 30 cm, so cut this out in the colour you need before you begin.

To prepare your pattern templates, use tracing paper and a pencil to transfer each one onto a piece of white paper, then cut it out.

Be inspired!

The step-by-step instructions are a guide to making each pirate. If you don't have all the items, or you want to dress the pirates differently, don't be afraid to experiment with the designs and materials. You can adapt each look to make your own versions of these buccaneering heroes of the high seas!

Top Tips

Follow these top tips to become a pirate-making expert and create perfect characters every time!

Keep both hands free to decorate your dolly pegs by standing them in a piece of sticky putty.

If you run out of tissue paper, use fabric scraps, coloured paper or even tinfoil.

Keep any offcuts to make your pirates' hats, shoes and accessories. Look for beads, sequins, buttons and scraps of ribbon to decorate your pirates.

Give each pirate a different expression. Angry, happy, fearsome and surprised are all good pirate looks … you decide!

Warning:
Fuzzy sticks and scissors have sharp points. Use under direct adult supervision.

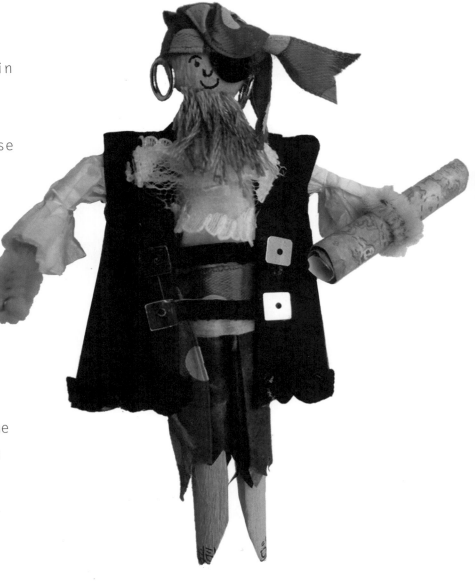

Aaargh!

Squawk!

You will need

- Half a pink fuzzy stick
- A dolly peg
- Glue
- Blue tissue paper, 30 x 30 cm
- Scissors
- Gold trim
- Sequins (round & square)
- A black pompom
- 1 m of grey thread
- A felt-tip pen
- Black card, 14.5 x 10.5 cm
- Two small pieces of feather
- A small piece of red tissue paper
- A green pompom
- A cocktail stick

1 Take half a pink fuzzy stick. Ask an adult to turn over the ends to make the hands. Stick it to the back of the dolly peg to create the arms.

2 Cut the square of blue tissue paper in half. Measure and cut out two 5 cm squares from one of the pieces. Glue one square to the edge of one of the dolly peg's legs and wrap it around.

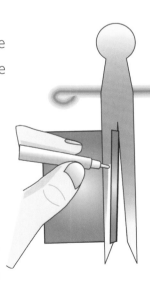

3 Pleat the other 5 cm square of tissue paper, and then ask an adult to cut it in half to make pantaloons. Take one of the pleated rectangles and stick it around the waist and knee, gathering it in as you go around. Repeat on the other leg with the other half of pleated tissue paper. You now have one good leg and one peg leg!

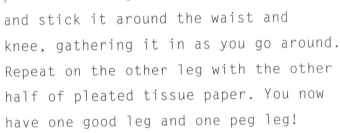

4 Fold the rest of this piece of blue tissue paper in half. Put the top of pattern piece (A) onto the folded edge of tissue paper and draw around it. Cut this out to make the pirate's tunic.

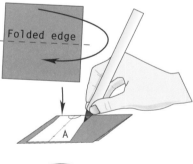
Folded edge

A

5 Pull the tunic gently over the head and glue the edges together. Wind gold trim around the bottom of the pantaloons and glue in place. Then, stick gold trim and sequins to the front.

8 For the shoe, stick the black pompom onto the base of the blue-covered leg and add a square sequin for the buckle.

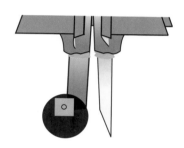

6 To make the pirate's jacket, turn to page 10 and follow the instructions for Blackbeard's jacket, but use pattern piece (H) and the remaining piece of blue tissue paper.

*Note: You can fold over the tissue paper twice to give a double-layered jacket.

9 Take the grey thread and cut it in half. Fold over one half and repeat until you have the desired length of hair, before gluing it to the dolly peg's head. Fold over the remaining length and stick it onto the face to create a beard. Ask an adult to neaten the ends with scissors.

7 Put the jacket onto your pirate and glue the sides together. Decorate the jacket with any spare gold trim and sequins.

10 Use a felt-tip pen to draw the pirate's features.

11 To make the pirate's hat, you will need pattern piece (C) and the black card. Copy the pattern onto the black card and cut it out. Ask an adult to help cut out the hole in the centre.

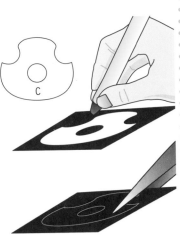

12 Fold your hat in half and decorate it with a small piece of feather, a sequin and spare gold trim.

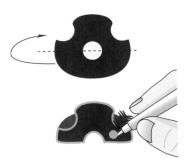

13 Glue your finished hat to the head.

* Remember to keep your pattern pieces safe as you will need them to make your other pirates' clothes.

14 To make the parrot, you will need a scrap of red tissue paper, a green pompom, a square sequin and a piece of black feather.

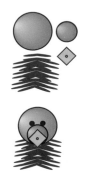

15 Stick the piece of red tissue paper to the front of the pompom. Then, stick the square sequin to this. Draw two eyes with the felt-tip pen above the beak and attach the piece of feather to the back. Finally, stick the parrot on Long John's shoulder.

16 Use the cocktail stick to make Long John Silver a crutch!

Arghh!

You will need
- Half a pink fuzzy stick
- A dolly peg
- Glue
- Black tissue paper, 30 x 30 cm
- Scissors
- Black twine
- Silver sequins (round & square)
- Black card, 14.5 x 10.5 cm
- A piece of tinfoil
- A scrap of lace
- 1 m of black thread
- A felt-tip pen
- A cocktail stick

1 Take half a pink fuzzy stick. Ask an adult to turn over the ends to make the hands. Stick it to the back of the dolly peg to create the arms.

3 To make the tunic, turn to page 5 and follow the instructions for Long John's tunic, using the rest of the piece of black tissue paper. Open the tunic out and snip halfway up the middle of one side and fold back the edges.

Folded edge

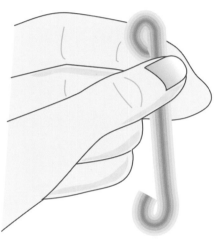

2 Cut the square of black tissue paper in half. Measure and cut out two 5 cm squares of tissue paper from one of the pieces. Glue one square to the edge of one of the dolly peg's legs, wrap it around and glue the edge down. Repeat this step for the other leg.

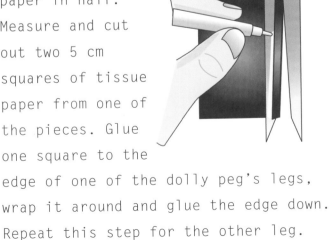

4 Pull the tunic gently over the head and glue the edges together. Wind black twine around the waist and glue in place. Then, stick on a silver square sequin for the belt buckle.

*Note: Keep all of your scraps as they will come in handy later.

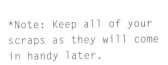

5 To make the boots, you will need pattern piece (D) and the black card. Measure and cut out two 6 x 8 cm rectangles from the card. Fold these in half along the short edge. Place pattern piece (D) along the folded edge and draw the pattern onto the card. Cut this out and repeat for the other boot.

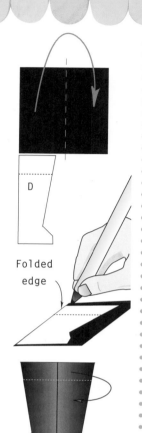

Folded edge

6 Fold over the top of the boots, then glue one around each leg.

7 Decorate the boots using tinfoil for the toecaps and sequins.

8 For the jacket you will need pattern piece (B). Fold the rest of the black tissue paper in half, then in half again. Put the top of pattern piece (B) onto the folded edge of the tissue paper, draw around it and cut it out.

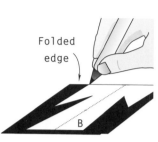

Folded edge

9 Open the jacket out and make a cut up the middle of one side and make a little snip on each side at the top. Now fold back the edges to make the lapels. Fold over the edges of the sleeves to create the cuffs. Gently place the jacket over the arms and glue the edges together.

10 Decorate the jacket with black twine and sequins. You can give the jacket frilly cuffs by using a little scrap lace or by scrunching up a little tissue paper and gluing it in place.

11 Take the black thread and cut it in half. Fold over one half and repeat until you have the desired length of hair, before gluing it to the dolly peg's head. Fold over the remaining length and stick it onto the face to create a beard. Trim the ends, leaving them slightly scruffy for Blackbeard's fearsome look.

12 Use a felt-tip pen to draw the pirate's features.

13 To make the pirate's hat, you will need pattern piece (F) and the black card. Copy the circle onto the card and cut it out. Then fold over the three semicircles on the pattern, place it on your circle of card and trace around the triangle.

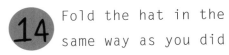

14 Fold the hat in the same way as you did the pattern, then pinch in all three corners. (Ask an adult to help as this can be a bit tricky.) Decorate it with small sequins and glue the hat to the head.

15 Use the cocktail stick to make Blackbeard a sword!

Shiver me timbers!

* Remember to keep your pattern pieces safe as you will need them to make your other pirates clothes.

You will need

- Half a brown fuzzy stick
- A dolly peg
- Glue
- Green tissue paper, 30 x 30 cm
- Scissors
- Gold trim
- Coloured ribbon (optional)
- Coloured thread (optional)
- Sequins (round & square)
- 1 m of red thread
- A felt-tip pen
- A lilac pompom
- A strip of white tissue paper
- Brown card, 14.5 x 10.5 cm
- Tinfoil

Barbarossa

1 Take half a brown fuzzy stick. Ask an adult to turn over the ends to make the hands. Stick it to the back of the dolly peg to create arms.

2 Cut the square of green tissue in half. Fold one of the pieces of green tissue in half. Using pattern piece (A) put the top of the pattern onto the folded edge of tissue paper and draw around it. For this tunic you will need to add an extra 1 cm to the length (so it looks like a dress).

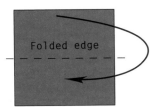

Folded edge

A

Folded edge

Extra length

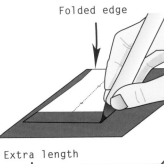

3 Pull the tunic gently over the head and glue the edges together. Wind gold trim around the waist several times to create a sash, then glue in place.

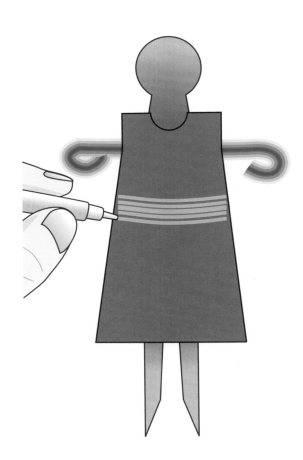

4 To make the pirate's jacket, turn to page 10 and follow the instructions for Blackbeard's jacket. Use the other piece of green tissue.

*Note: You can fold over the tissue paper twice to give a double-layered jacket.

5 Gently place the jacket over the arms and glue the edges together.

6 Decorate the jacket using gold trim around the bottom and the cuffs.

7 To create the sash, fold over a strip of tissue paper until you have a long, thin strip.

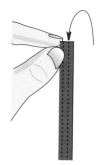

8 Wrap the sash around the body, securing it with glue. You can create tassels by gluing some pieces of thread together. Add a sequin as a buckle.

9 For the shoes, scrunch two pieces of tissue into balls and glue onto the base of the legs. Add a square sequin for each buckle.

10 Take the red thread and cut a small length off, enough to tie around the other threads.

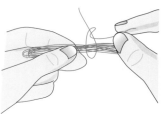

Take the single thread and tie it around the centre and secure with a knot. This will section the threads in two. Stick it onto the face to create a long beard. Ask an adult to neaten the ends with scissors.

11 Use a felt-tip pen to draw the pirate's features.

12 To make the turban, first glue the lilac pompom onto the head of the dolly peg. Then pleat a strip of white tissue paper.

13 Glue the end of the strip to the front of the pompom and wind the tissue around the head, securing it with glue at the front.

Add a sequin to the front of the turban as a jewel.

14 To make the cutlasses you will need pattern piece (G), a piece of brown card and tinfoil.

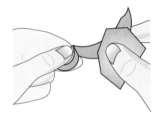

Copy the pattern onto the card twice and cut the shapes out. Wrap the tinfoil around each blade. Finally, place a cutlass in each of the pirate's hands.

Avast!

You will need

- Half a pink fuzzy stick
- A dolly peg
- Glue
- Black tissue paper, 30 x 30 cm
- Scissors
- White tissue paper, 30 x 30 cm
- A scrap of lace (optional)
- Black twine
- Silver sequins
  (round, square & hooped)
- Silver trim
- 1 m of red thread
- A felt-tip pen
- Black card, 14.5 x 10.5 cm
- A black pompom
- A small piece of black feather

1 Take half a pink fuzzy stick. Ask an adult to turn over the ends to make the hands. Stick it to the back of the dolly peg to create arms.

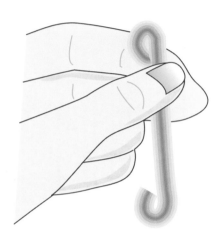

3 To make the shirt, you will need pattern piece (I) and the white tissue paper. Cut the tissue paper in half. Fold one of the pieces in half and put the top of pattern piece (I) onto the folded edge. Draw around it and cut it out.

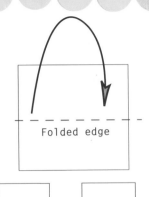

Folded edge

I

Folded edge

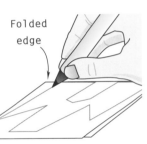

2 Cut the piece of black tissue paper in half. Measure and cut out two 5 cm squares of tissue paper from one of the pieces. Glue one square to the edge of the dolly peg's leg, wrap it around and glue the edge down. Repeat for the other leg.

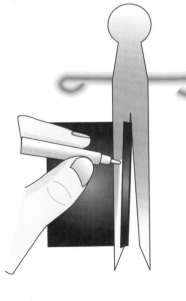

4 Pull the shirt gently over the head and glue the edges together. To make the ruffled front, scrunch up a piece of white tissue paper and glue in place. Or, if you have a piece of scrap lace, you can use this. Glue and wind black twine around the waist to create the bodice.

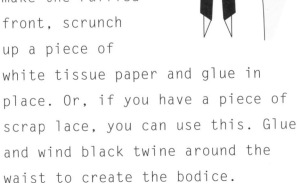

5 Stick a square sequin to the front of the bodice. Twist the ends of the shirt sleeves to make them appear ruffled.

*Note: You can tie and knot a piece of cotton around each sleeve end to hold them securely in place.

6 To make the boots, turn to page 10 and follow the instructions for Blackbeard's boots. Decorate the boots using scraps of twine and sequins.

7 For the waistcoat you will need pattern piece (K). Fold the black tissue in half. Put the top of pattern piece (K) onto the folded edge of tissue paper, draw around it and cut it out.

8 Open the waistcoat out and cut up the centre of one half. Then cut a rounded edge on both sides. Gently place the waistcoat over the arms and glue the edges together.

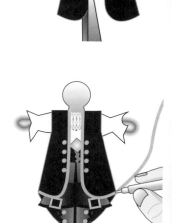

Decorate the edges of the waistcoat with silver trim. Stick on small sequins to look like buttons.

9 Take the red thread and fold it in half, then glue it to the dolly peg's head. Ask an adult to neaten the ends with scissors.

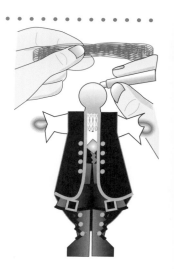

10 Stick two hooped sequins on either side of the head to look like earrings.

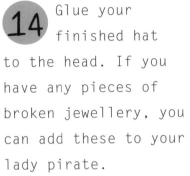

11 Use a felt-tip pen to draw on the pirate's features. Add some eyelashes to make her look like a woman.

12 To make the pirate's hat, you will need pattern piece (E) and the black card. Copy the circle onto the card and cut it out. Ask an adult to help cut out the hole in the centre.

13 Glue the black pompom in the centre of the hat over the hole. Wrap a piece of black twine around the base of the pompom and stick on a square sequin for the buckle. Then fold up both sides of the hat and add a small piece of black feather.

14 Glue your finished hat to the head. If you have any pieces of broken jewellery, you can add these to your lady pirate.

We have added a necklace chain and cross!

Aye, me beauty!

You will need
- Half a pink fuzzy stick
- A dolly peg
- Glue
- Brown tissue paper, 30 x 30 cm
- Scissors
- White tissue paper, 30 x 30 cm
- Brown card, 14.5 x 10.5 cm
- Sequins (3 x gold squares)
- 1 m of brown thread
- A small piece of red tissue paper
- A felt-tip pen
- A piece of brown fuzzy stick
- White paint
- A small paintbrush

Calico Jack

1 Take half a pink fuzzy stick. Ask an adult to turn over the ends to make the hands. Stick it to the back of the dolly peg to create arms.

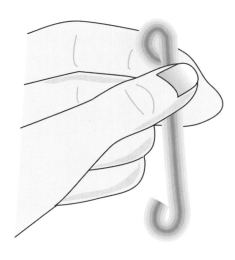

2 Cut the square of brown tissue paper in half. Measure and cut out two 5 cm squares from one of the pieces. Glue one square to the edge of the dolly peg's leg, wrap it around and glue the edge down. Repeat for the other leg.

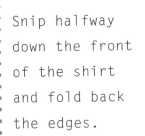

3 To make the shirt, you will need pattern piece (I) and the white tissue paper. Cut the tissue paper in half. Fold one of the pieces in half and put the top of pattern piece (I) onto the folded edge. Draw around it and cut it out.

Snip halfway down the front of the shirt and fold back the edges.

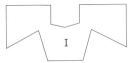

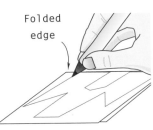

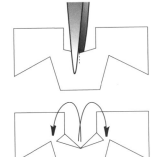

4 Pull the shirt gently over the head and glue the edges. Twist the ends of the shirt sleeves to make them ruffled.

*Note: You can tie and knot a piece of cotton around each sleeve end to hold them securely in place.

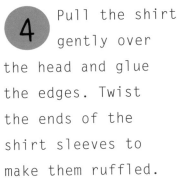

5 Fold the rest of this piece of brown tissue in half. Put the top of pattern piece (A) onto the folded edge of tissue and trace around it. Cut this out.

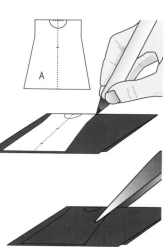

6 Open the tunic out and cut up the middle. Fold back the edges to make the lapels. Then snip off a little triangle from the bottom of each lapel.

7 Place the tunic over the arms and glue the edges together. To create the sash, fold over a strip of white tissue until you have a long, thin strip. Tie it around the waist.

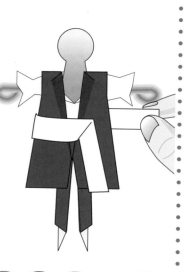

8 Cut a strip of brown card for the belt and glue this over the sash. Finish with a square sequin buckle.

9 To make the boots, you will need pattern piece (M) and the brown card. Measure and cut two 6 cm squares from the card. Fold these in half along the short edge.

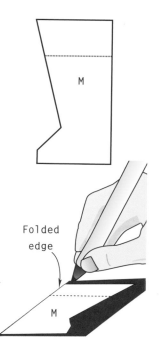

Folded edge

10 Place pattern piece (M) along the folded edge and copy the pattern onto the card. Cut this out and repeat for the other boot. Fold over the top of each boot,

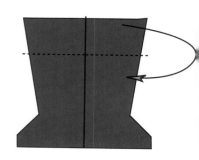

11 Glue one boot around each leg. Stick a square sequin to the front of each boot for a buckle.

12 Take the brown thread and fold it in half, then glue it to the dolly peg's head. Ask an adult to neaten the ends with scissors. Glue the offcuts on the face for the beard and moustache. Use a felt-tip pen to draw on the pirate's features.

13 To make the bandana, first pleat a strip of red tissue paper. Then, wrap it around the head and glue in place. We have added some beads to Jack's hair, but you can always use little bits of rolled up tissue and glue them on.

14 Copy the flag on page 32 onto a rectangle of black card, using the white paint and paintbrush. Let it dry, then glue it onto the piece of brown fuzzy stick. Place it in Jack's hand.

Ahoy there, Captain Jack!

You will need
- Half a pink fuzzy stick
- A dolly peg
- Glue
- Red tissue paper, 30 x 30 cm
- A scrap of white tissue paper
- A scrap of lace (optional)
- Scissors
- Gold trim
- Sequins (round and square)
- Brown card, 14.5 x 10.5 cm
- 1 m of black thread
- A felt-tip pen
- Red card, 14.5 x 10.5 cm
- A small piece of black feather

1 Take half a pink fuzzy stick. Ask an adult to turn over the ends to make the hands. Stick it to the back of the dolly peg to create arms.

2 Cut the square of red tissue paper in half. Measure and cut out two 5 cm squares from one of the pieces. Glue one square to the edge of the dolly peg's leg, wrap it around and glue the edge down. Repeat for the other leg.

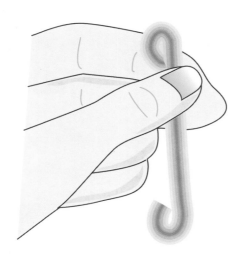

3 For the jacket you will need pattern piece (H). Fold the rest of the red tissue in half, then in half again. Put the top of pattern piece (H) onto the folded edge, draw around it and cut it out.

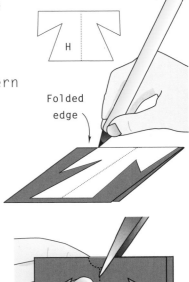

Snip a little way down the front of the jacket and fold back the edges.

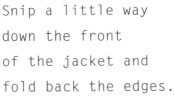

4 Pull the jacket gently over the head and glue the edges. To make the ruffled front, scrunch up a piece of white tissue paper and glue to the front. Or, if you have a piece of scrap lace, you can use this.

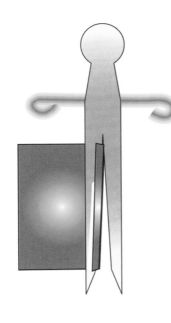

5 You can give the jacket frilly cuffs by using a little scrap lace or by scrunching up a little tissue paper and gluing it in place. Decorate the jacket with gold trim and sequins.

Copy the pattern onto the card. Cut this out and repeat for the other boot.

6 Cut a strip of brown card for the belt and wrap it around the waist, pulling in the tissue. Glue in place. Finish with a square sequin buckle.

8 Fold over the top of each boot, then snip up the back of each boot, folding back the flaps. Wrap a boot around each leg and glue to the front. Overlap the folded tops and glue in place. Stick a square sequin to the front of each boot as a buckle. To finish, add gold trim to the top of the boots.

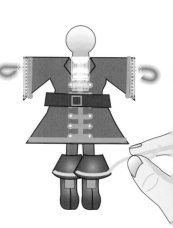

7 To make the boots, you will need pattern piece (M) and brown card. Measure and cut out two 6 cm squares from the card. Fold these in half along the short edge. Place pattern piece (M) along the folded edge.

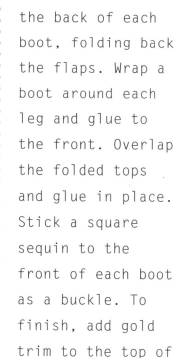

Folded edge

M

9 Take the black thread and ask an adult to cut a small piece from one end for the moustache. Fold the rest of the thread in half and repeat until you have the desired length of hair, before gluing it to the dolly peg's head.

Take the small length of thread and fold it until you have a long moustache. Glue it to the face, then glue the ends together to create a goatee beard. Ask an adult to neaten the ends of the thread.

10 Use a felt-tip pen to draw on the pirate's features.

11 To make the pirate's hat, you will need pattern piece (J) and the red card. Copy the pattern onto the red card and cut it out. Ask an adult to help cut out the hole in the centre.

*Note: if you don't have any red card, you can colour a piece of card with paint or felt-tip pen.

12 Fold your hat in half and decorate it with a small piece of feather, a sequin and spare gold trim. Then glue your finished hat to the head.

We have added a small bottle of pirate's rum. You can make one using a piece of tinfoil.

Drink up me hearties, yo ho!

You will need

- Half a pink fuzzy stick
- A dolly peg
- Glue
- Blue tissue paper, 30 x 30 cm
- Scissors
- White tissue paper, 30 x 30 cm
- A piece of red tissue or ribbon
- Black tissue paper, 30 x 30 cm
- Black twine
- Sequins (square, circled and hooped)
- 1 m of grey thread
- A felt-tip pen
- Brown card 14.5 x 10.5 cm

1 Take half a pink fuzzy stick. Ask an adult to turn over the ends to make the hands. Stick it to the back of the dolly peg to create arms.

2 Cut the square of blue tissue paper in half. Measure and cut out two 5 cm squares from one of the pieces. Then, cut a ragged edge along the bottom. Glue one square to the edge of the dolly peg's leg, wrap it around and glue the edge down. Repeat for the other leg.

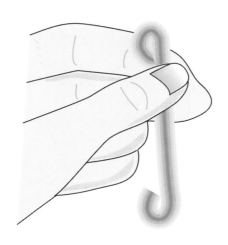

3 To make the shirt, turn to page 21 and follow the instructions for Jack's shirt. To make the ruffled front, scrunch up a piece of white tissue paper and glue to the front. Or, if you have a piece of scrap lace, you can use this.

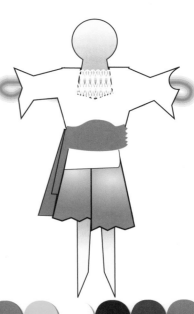

4 To create the sash, fold over a strip of red tissue paper until you have a long, thin strip. Tie it around the waist and let the tails hang to one side. Leave one longer than the other.

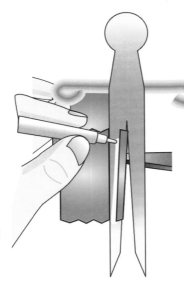

5 To make the waistcoat, cut the black tissue paper in half. Fold one of the pieces of black tissue paper in half. Put the top of pattern piece (A) onto the folded edge of tissue and trace around it. Cut this out.

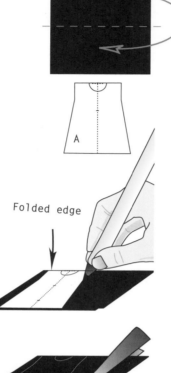

Folded edge

6 Open the waistcoat out and cut up the middle. Fold back the edges to make the lapels.

7 Gently place the tunic over the arms and glue the edges together. Cut two strips of black twine, glue them across the front and add two sequins either side, as buckles.

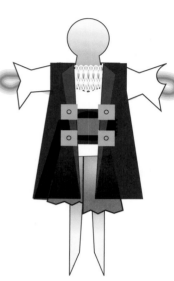

8 To make the bandana, first pleat a strip of red tissue paper. Then, glue one end to the head, wrap it around and glue the end in place.

*Note: if you are using a piece of ribbon, tie a knot and leave the tails hanging out the side.

9 Take the grey thread, fold it in half and repeat until you have the desired length of beard, before gluing it to the dolly peg's face. Ask an adult to neaten the ends with scissors.

10 Use a felt-tip pen to draw on the pirate's features. Stick on a little piece of black tissue for the eyepatch.

11 To finish your pirate, add two gold hooped sequins for earrings and a tiny piece of rolled up paper for a treasure map.

The booty's all mine!

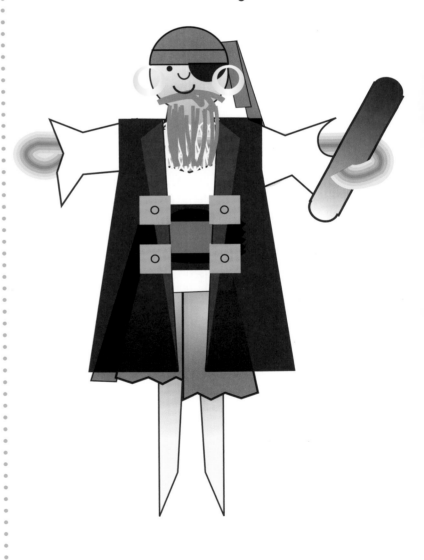

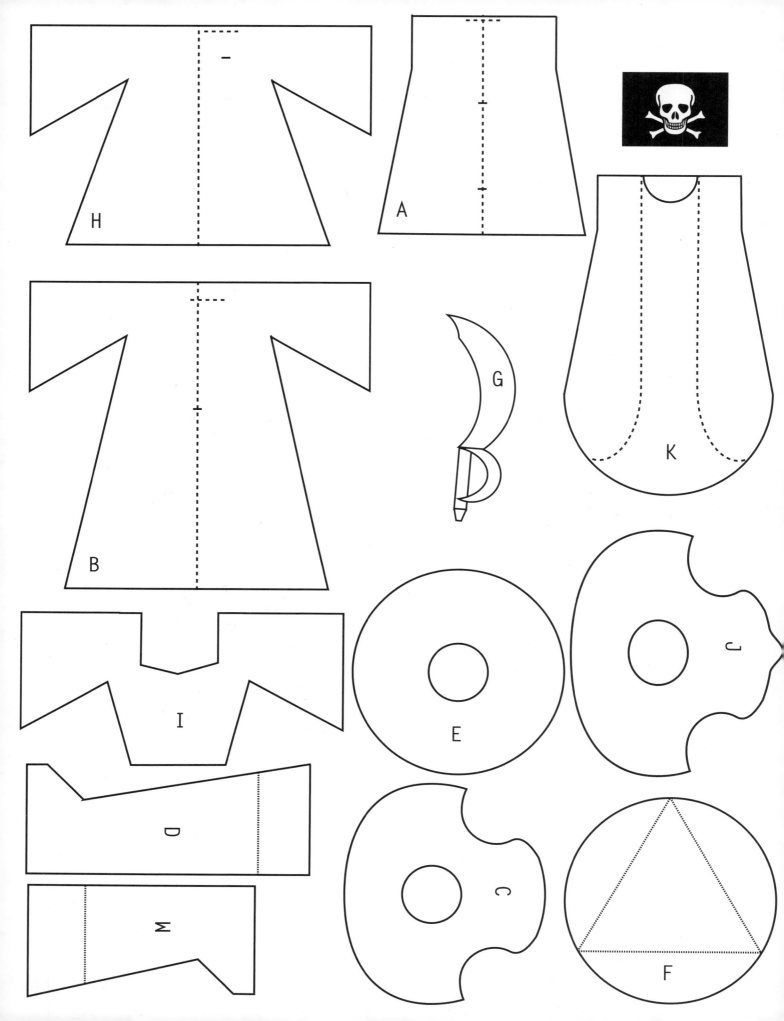